Ernst **Pietà or Revolution by Night**

ISBN 0 946590 23 0
Published by order of the Trustees 1986

Designed and published by Tate Gallery Publications,
Millbank, London SW1P 4RG
Printed by Balding + Mansell Limited, Wisbech

MALCOLM GEE

Ernst **Pietà** or Revolution by Night

THE TATE GALLERY

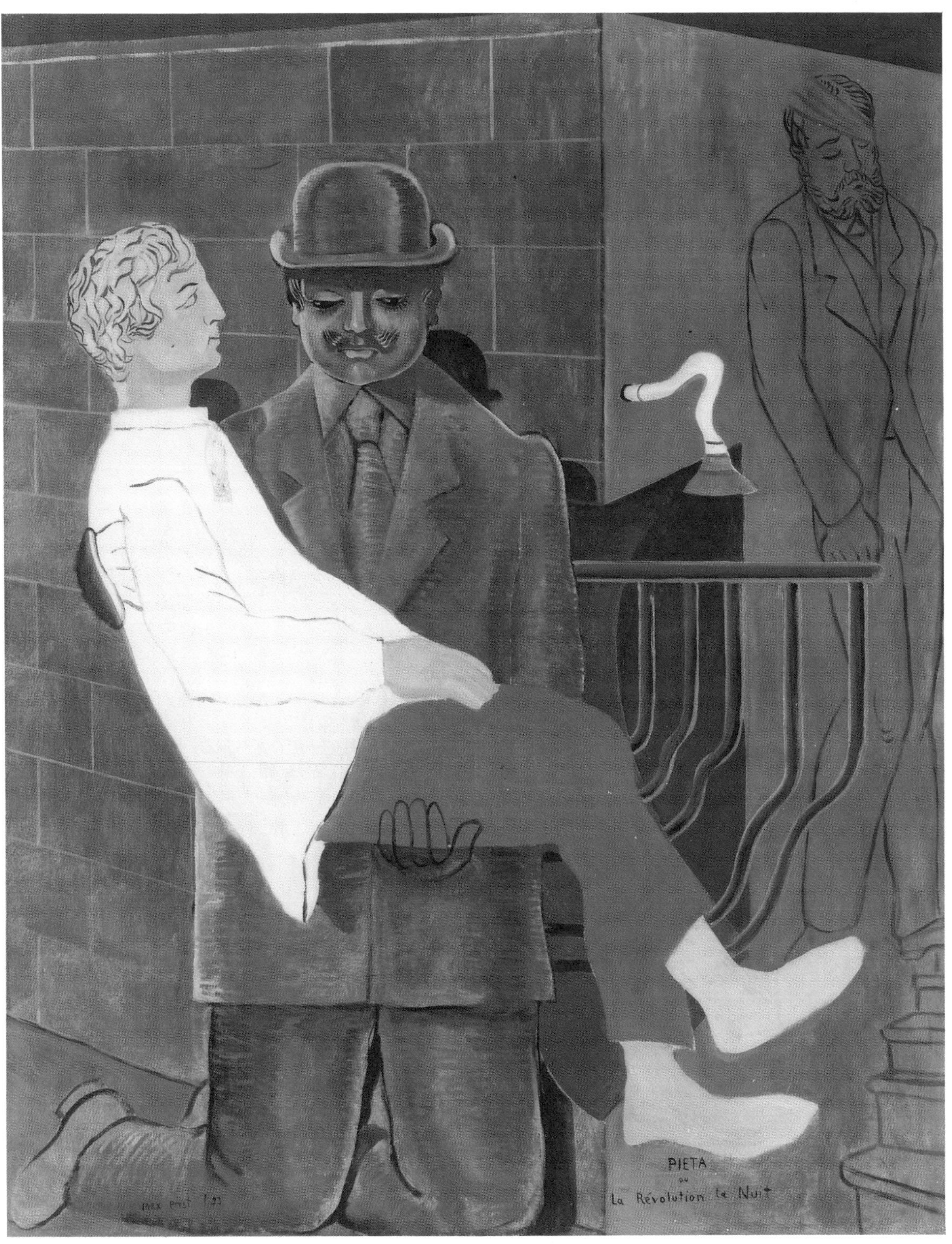

Max Ernst, **Pietà or Revolution by Night** 1923
oil on canvas, 116 × 88.5 cm, purchased by the Tate Gallery in 1981

Foreword

With the acquisition of 'Pietà or Revolution by Night', the Tate Gallery now owns what is probably the finest group of Max Ernst's early Surrealist paintings to be found anywhere in the world. In 1960 the Gallery purchased 'Of This Men shall know Nothing' 1923, which had once belonged to André Breton, the high priest of Surrealism, himself; its most recent owner, however, was the second generation Surrealist painter, Gordon Onslow-Ford. Fifteen years later the no less enigmatic 'Celebes' 1921, Ernst's first large oil painting, became available. Like 'Pietà', it had an impeccable provenance: the poet Paul Eluard until 1938, thereafter the late Sir Roland Penrose, who did more than anyone to introduce Surrealism to Britain. We shall be republishing Sir Roland's Charlton Lecture on 'Celebes' as a booklet later in this series.

Ernst was deeply interested in Freudian ideas and familiar with actual case histories; at one time he even considered taking up psychiatry as a profession. In the essay which follows, Malcolm Gee argues that Ernst's reading of a particularly well-known essay by Freud enabled him, in 'Pietà', to symbolise his own traumatic relationship with his father. We are indebted to Dr Gee for providing a key to this puzzling but unforgettable picture and for shedding fresh light on the rich and fascinating Surrealist mentality. We would also like to thank Günter Metken for his help in obtaining illustrations.

Richard Calvocoressi
Assistant keeper, Modern Collection

Ernst **Pietà ou la Revolution la Nuit**

Twentieth-century art is frequently difficult to understand and interpret. The modern painters whose work we now value most highly have considered the development of a personal vision, and the radical exploration of colour and form, to be more important than making their work easily intelligible to others. The fact that 'Pietà or Revolution by Night' is hard to comprehend is not therefore unusual in itself. But, this painting, like others by Max Ernst from the period 1919–24, does stand out by the particular nature of the difficulties which it poses the viewer. It is not formally innovative – indeed on this level, at which aesthetic interest usually lies, it is rather banal. Moreover, the contents do not, in themselves, display any great powers of invention or imagination. Unlike 'The Bride Stripped Bare by her Bachelors, Even', by Marcel Duchamp, which presents a secret drama enacted by inhuman protagonists, the 'Pietà' represents easily distinguishable figures and objects: a man in a bowler hat holding a youth; a staircase by a wall; a third, bearded, figure with a bandaged head. However, although these things are easy to see, they are almost impossible to make sense of. The meaning of the painting is as elusive as that of Duchamp's 'Bride'. This tension between the obvious nature of the presentation and its absent, or hidden, significance is a central factor in the fascination which the picture undoubtedly exerts. It appears as an illustration, but of an unknown text. Who are these men and what are the relations between them? This is the immediate question which scrutiny of the work gives rise to, and the present essay is largely concerned with answering it. In doing so, it will also seek to explain why Max Ernst should have made such a painting, and why it is a 'modern masterpiece'.

The evolution of a painter poet

The 'Pietà' is one of a series of paintings which Ernst began in Cologne in 1921 with the 'Elephant from Celebes' and ended in Paris in 1924 with 'Two Children are threatened by a Nightingale'. These works, which include 'Oedipus Rex', 'At the First Plain Word' and 'Woman, Old Man and Flower', use a similar precise, rather dull, technique to represent scenes which startle the viewer through their dislocated and often absurd character. They are the culmination of the first major phase of Max Ernst's career, during which he established the general principles

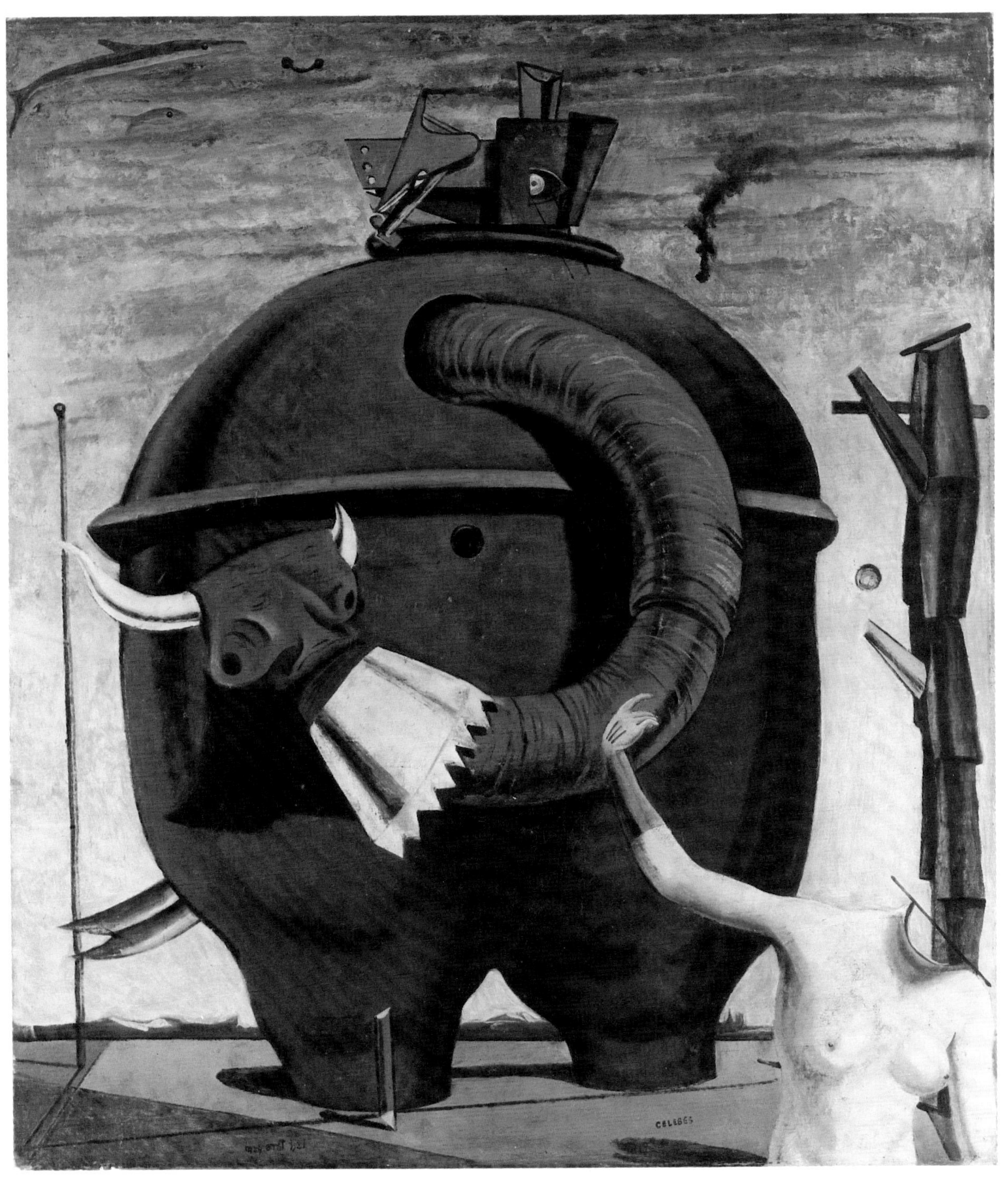

1 **Celebes** 1921, *Tate Gallery*

of his artistic philosophy and developed a number of the themes and technical practices which he was to use throughout his life.[1] Although two important paintings in the series, 'Celebes' and 'Oedipus Rex', were made in Cologne, most of them were produced in Paris, where he moved in the autumn of 1922. This move was of considerable material and symbolic significance: through it he became a member of the nascent Surrealist circle and completed his rejection of the constraints of patriotism, class, and conventional morality which his background had imposed on him. The uncompromising spirit in which he did so, and the complexities of feeling which accompanied this revolt, are directly reflected in these paintings, and in the 'Pietà' perhaps above all.

Ernst achieved some recognition as a painter before the war, when he was living in Bonn. He met August Macke in 1910 or 1911, and became an active member of the group of local artists who were concerned with introducing modern ideas to the region. At that time painting was not a full time professional occupation for him. Partly because his family wanted him to pursue a secure career, but also because it suited his temperament, he was registered as a student in philosophy at the University of Bonn. Although he fairly rapidly abandoned orthodox learning and the professional perspectives which it opened up, this period of study was influential in his development and is significant for an understanding of his work. Like Marcel Duchamp, his approach to art was self-aware and cerebral. He came to be interested in the relationship between art and the irrational, and eventually sought to remove the conscious, deliberate, aspect of picture making from his work almost entirely. But even in doing so (and the extent to which he actually did was limited) he remained an intellectual artist. Making art was for him a form of enquiry rather than the pursuit of a purely aesthetic goal. Many of his works, although they possess an undoubted poetic quality, need to be viewed also as propositions of a rather special kind, which articulate a specific, disruptive, view of society and the self. The basis of this view was established during his years in Bonn, when he was influenced by the ideas of Nietzsche, Stirner and Freud, amongst others.[2] His painting at this time was still rather tentative, although it showed an acute awareness of the main currents of the international avant-garde. Immediately after the war, however, he embarked on a series of works which clearly embodied the iconoclastic tenor of his thinking. 'On the 1st of August 1914 M.E. died. He was resurrected on the 11th of November 1918 as a young man who aspired to find the myths of his time.'[3] From this point on, he devoted himself entirely to art, but broke with the current orthodoxy of even *avant-garde* expressionist painting. In the current of Dada, he produced images of a provocative, humorous, and illogical nature which challenged virtually all accepted criteria of aesthetic judgement. Their central feature was the use of the technique and principle of collage – 'The miracle of the total transfiguration of beings and objects with or without modification

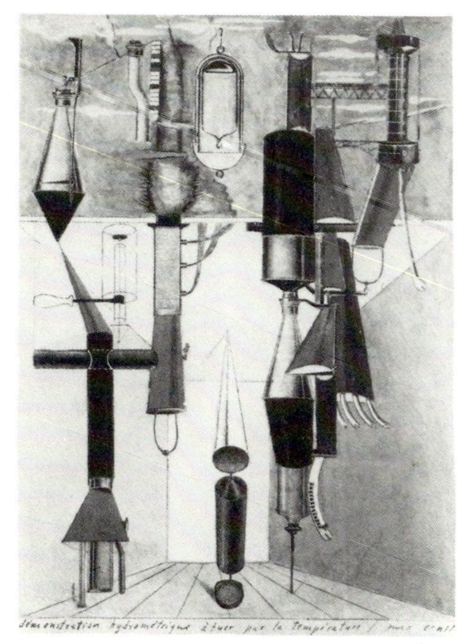

2 **Démonstration hydrométrique à tuer par la température** 1920
collage and gouache,
Private Collection, Paris

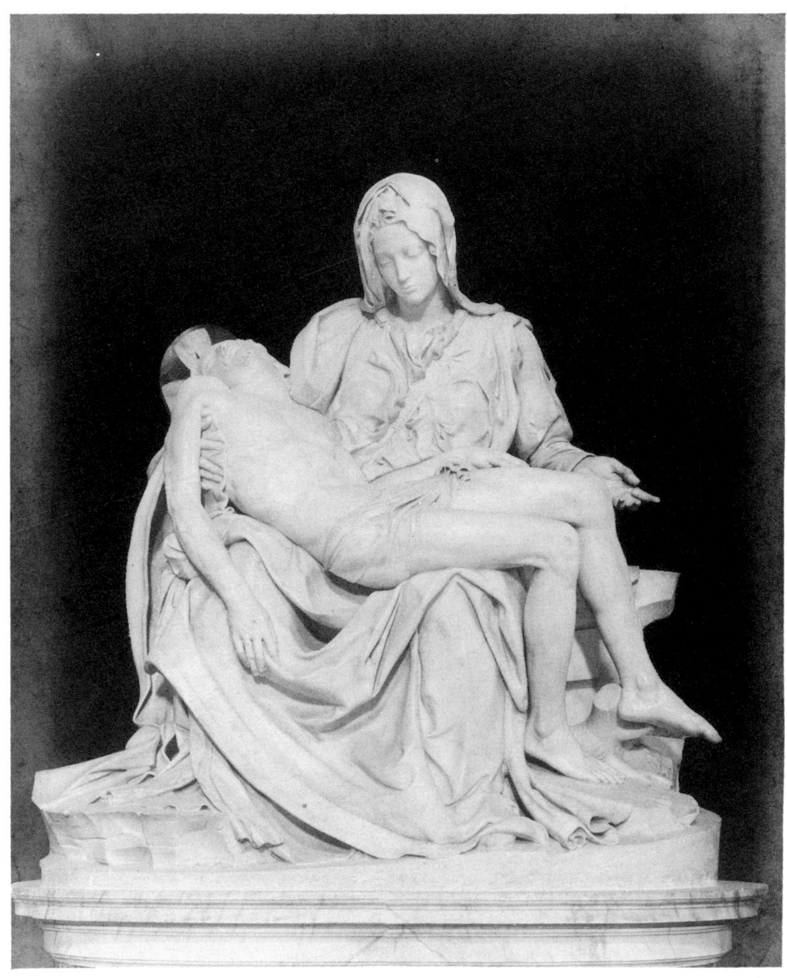

3 Michelangelo, **Pietà**
St Peter's, Rome

of their physical or anatomical aspect.'[4] Ernst took images from sources such as technical journals and mail order catalogues and altered them so that their original meaning was obscured, giving way to a shifting, allusive, play of reference which was often made more dense by the addition of a humorous inscription. The basic idea of collage as he conceived it – to take a found image and inject it with a new, strange, identity by abstracting it from its original context and confronting it with a new one – was a driving force in all his work between 1919 and 1924. After 1925 the actual technique was overshadowed by his discovery of 'frottage' (rubbing), but it re-emerged dramatically in 1929 when he used it to produce his novel *La femme 100 têtes*. Two of the paintings of the 1921–4 series, 'Celebes' and 'Oedipus Rex', derived directly from a collage idea.[5] The 'Pietà' did not, but it relates to the collage principle in at least one way. The central image is an adaptation of a traditional element of Christian iconography. The painting therefore functions to some extent in a similar way to a collage, using another art object as source – Michelangelo's sculpture in St Peter's is a famous example that Ernst may have had in mind. An important feature of collage is that it not only transforms the found element itself, but also subverts, by implication, the context from which it is drawn. Just as the precise, ordered, world of the technical journal loses its stability in Ernst's early collages, so, in the 'Pietà', the sacred aura of Christian art becomes infected with the grotesque. Ernst frequently employed this device both to attack religion and to suggest that art related to primal feelings rather than to elevated sentiments. He transformed Parmigianino's 'Madonna' into a spanker, and Leonardo's 'Virgin with St Anne' into a 'night of love'. In December 1922 he used it to make private fun of his father: his painting 'The Rendez-Vous of Friends' was loosely based on Raphael's fresco the 'Dispute over the Sacraments'. Max Ernst's father had once made a copy of this work, incorporating local acquaintances among the figures. His son's picture shows himself surrounded by his new 'family' – the Surrealists.[6]

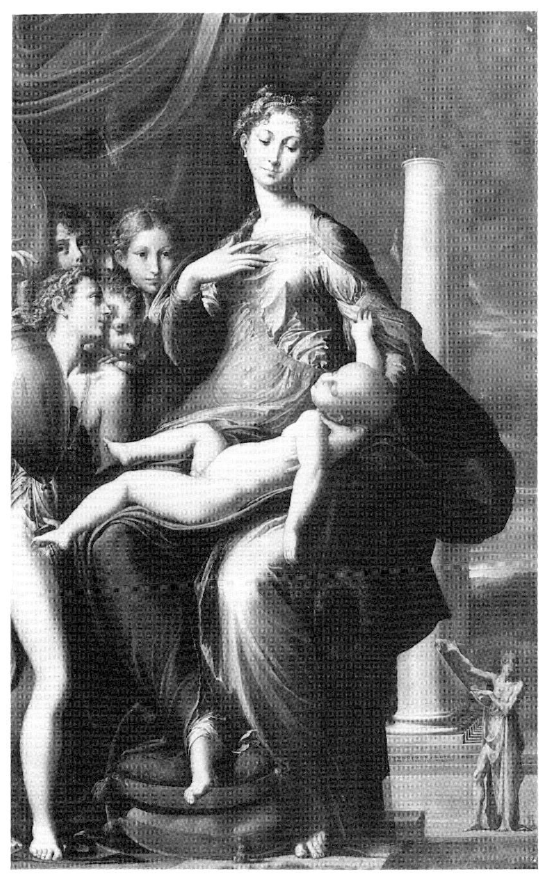

4 Parmigianino, **Madonna col collo lungo**
Galleria degli Uffizi, Florence

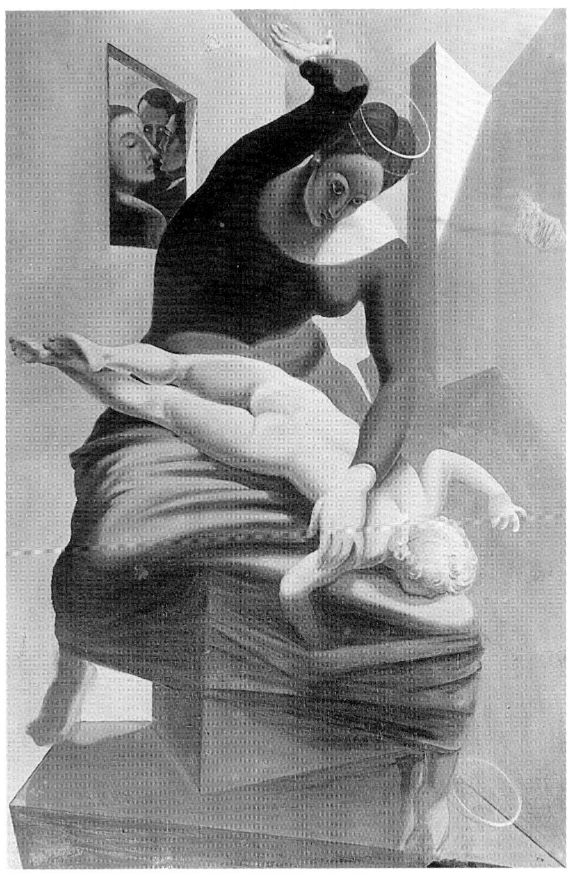

5 **The Virgin Mary spanking the infant Jesus in front of three Witnesses: André Breton, Paul Eluard and the artist** 1926
Private Collection, Brussels

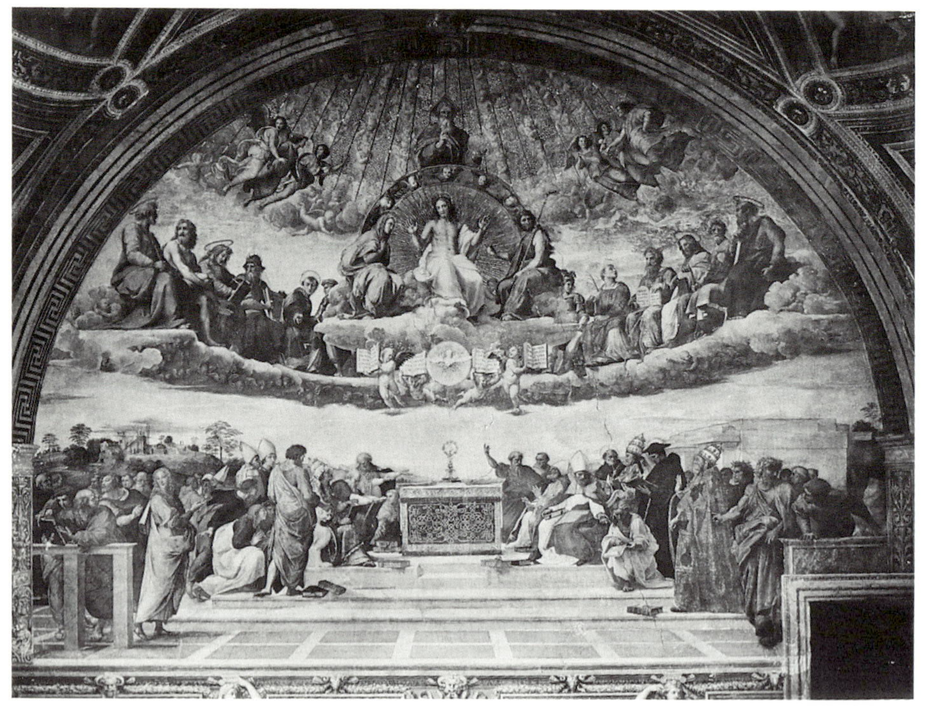

6 Raphael, **Disputà**
Stanza della Segnatura, the Vatican, Rome

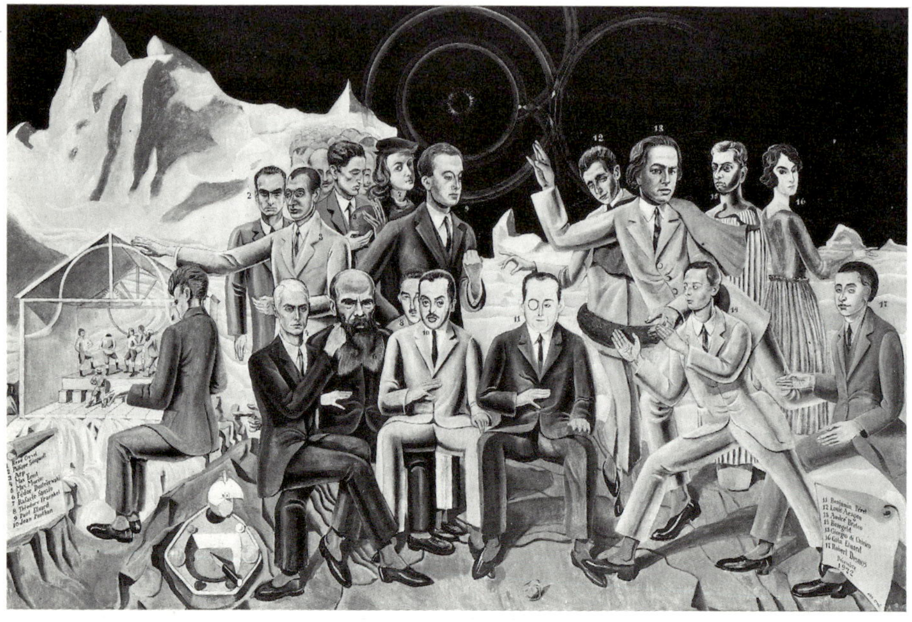

7 **Au rendez-vous des amis (The Rendez-Vous of Friends)**
Wallraf-Richartz-Museum, Cologne

Surrealism

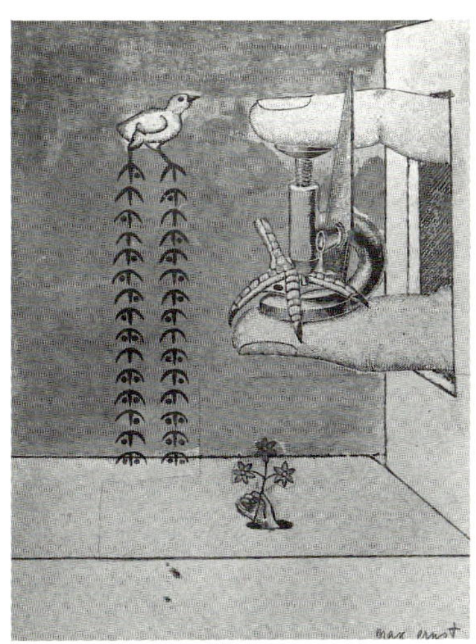

8 **L'invention** *or* **L'oiseau de l'infini** 1921, collage and gouache (used in Paul Eluard, *Répétitions*, Paris, 1922) *Private Collection, Paris*

The Surrealist movement did not assume a public existence until 1924, with the publication of the *Manifesto of Surrealism* by André Breton and the first issue of *La Révolution Surréaliste*. These events represented, however, the culmination of several years of collective experience and reflection on the part of a group of young writers in Paris who had first worked together in the context of Dada in 1919 and whose ideas had evolved during the period 1921–24 away from the violent anarchic humour of Dada towards a more coherent, organised, statement of cultural and social revolt. Max Ernst had become involved with this group, centred around André Breton, Louis Aragon, and Paul Eluard, over a year before he actually moved to Paris. They had become aware of his work through Tristan Tzara, the animator of Dada in Zurich, who settled in Paris early in 1920. In the spring of 1921 they invited him to exhibit at the Galerie Sans Pareil. According to André Breton, Ernst's collages struck them as a 'revelation'. That autumn he met both Breton and Eluard – in November Paul and Gala Eluard, disappointed at missing the Ernsts on holiday in the Tyrol, visited them in Cologne. An exceptional rapport developed between the two men: Eluard bought 'Celebes' and 'Oedipus Rex', selected collages to illustrate *Répétitions*, and invited Ernst to collaborate on another book, which appeared in

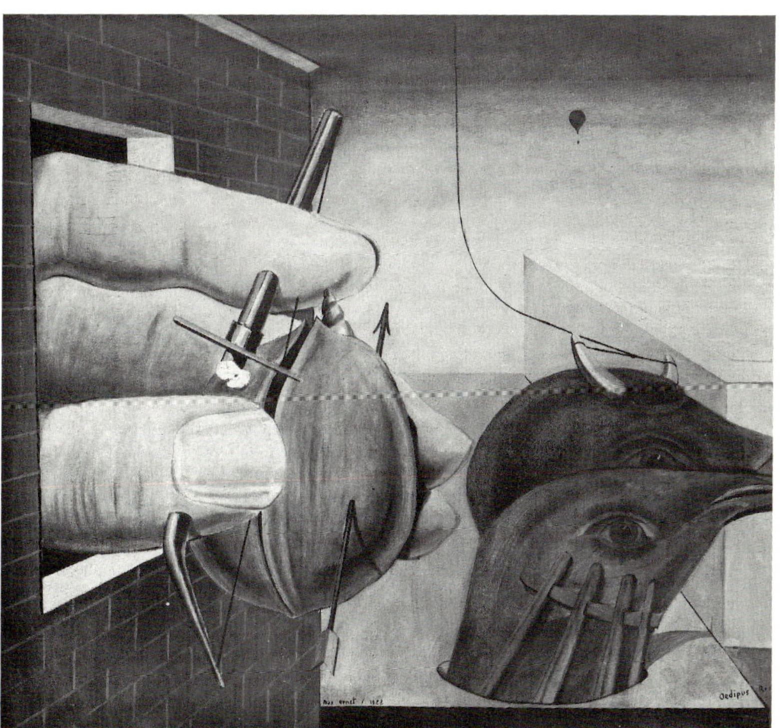

9 **Oedipus Rex** 1922
Private Collection, Paris

1922 under the title *Les Malheurs des Immortels*. Ernst was already thinking of leaving Cologne for Paris: when he finally did, alone, in the autumn of 1922, he went to live with the Eluards.[7] He was immediately plunged into an atmosphere of collective experiment and investigation: the group had revived the practice of automatic writing, and were excited by the effects of producing it in a trance. In the account of their sessions which Breton published that November, Ernst was cited as one of the seven central participants.[8]

The manifesto of 1924 is famous for hardly mentioning the visual arts at all. Surrealism was an idea that related first to writing, and then to the entire field of cultural and social action. Only two of the figures in 'The Rendez-Vous of Friends', de Chirico and Ernst himself, were painters with a direct relation to the Surrealist circle, and de Chirico was already suspected of 'betraying' the qualities of his early work.[9] Although other painters – notably Masson, Miró, Tanguy and Dalí – were associated with the Surrealists at various points, Ernst's position in relation to the movement was unique. He was virtually the only visual artist in the 1920s who consistently accepted the Surrealist position for his own work, and was prepared to sacrifice the traditional concerns of the painter – composition, touch, palette – in the interest of the 'total revision of values' which Surrealism called for. Already in 1922 he no longer considered himself 'a painter' – the encounter with Breton and his friends provided him with exactly the intellectual environment which suited his temperament and convictions. Although they rejected orthodox criteria for judging it, Breton and Eluard, in particular, acknowledged the power of visual art. They were impressed by Ernst because he combined an astonishing sense of imagery with a lucidity and intellectual curiosity which matched their own.[10]

The chief objective of the Surrealist group in 1922 and 1923 was to explore the creative faculties of the mind in total freedom. They argued that the conventions of literature and art, and the moral rules of bourgeois society, imprisoned it and rendered it sterile. They were fascinated by figures such as the Marquis de Sade and Lautréamont, who had dared to think outside the 'bounds of reason'. Naturally, they were also interested in the idea of the unconscious mind, and a large part of their efforts were specifically devoted to finding ways of externalising it directly. They had two models for this: automatic writing and dreams. In fact, dreams are an exemplary form of 'psychic automatism' and Breton's famous definition of Surrealism in the 1924 manifesto included a reference to the 'omnipotence of the dream'.[11] One of the reasons why Breton and Eluard were enthusiastic about painting was that it could evoke the intensity and surprise of the dream experience more powerfully than writing. Max Ernst knew this, and he set out to recreate the qualities of dream imagery in his work. To do so, he drew on his knowledge of Freud.

Freud

The Surrealists were, not surprisingly, interested in the ideas of Freud. In the summer of 1921, after André and Simone Breton had met Ernst in the Tyrol, they visited Vienna with the Eluards, where Breton had an interview with Freud. The manifesto acknowledged the importance of his work on dreams, and the first issue of *La Révolution Surréaliste* included him in its collective portrait of male dreamers. In the 1930s Gradiva, the subject of a famous essay by Freud on the parallels between art and psychoanalysis, became a mythical Surrealist heroine, painted by Dali and Masson. However, their first hand knowledge of his writing was extemely limited, partly because it was only translated into French with considerable delay, and partly because its technical aspects did not greatly interest them. Breton seized on the fact that a scientist had demonstrated the preponderant role played by the unconscious in human life, and used it to justify his own ideas about language and the imagination, but, at least initially he did not concern himself with Freud's specific theories concerning repression and the mechanism of dreams. Max Ernst had a different position. He had read several major texts by Freud – *The Interpretation of Dreams* and *Jokes and their Relationship to the Unconscious* were known to his circle of friends in Bonn before the war, at a time when he was directly concerned with psychiatry. Later, he found the ideas of psychoanalysis suggestive for the task which he set himself as an artist. He also seems to have considered them interesting in terms of his own personality and experiences.

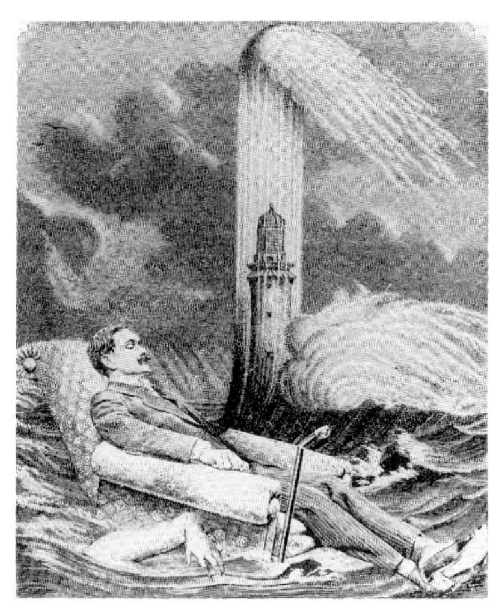

10 **Quiétude**, collage from *La femme 100 têtes*, Paris 1929

Ernst made frequent, sometimes playful, use of typical 'Freudian' symbols throughout the 1920s. The pointed branches and curled trunk of 'Celebes', and the lighthouse flooded by a column of water in 'Quiétude' are clearly informed by the catalogue of phallic imagery contained in *The Interpretation of Dreams*. A number of works use specific essays as source material. Werner Spies has shown that 'At the First Plain Word' is, in part, an illustration of a dream sequence in *Dreams and Delusions in Jensen's Gradiva*; Geoffrey Hinton has argued that 'Of This Men shall know Nothing' draws on the case of President Schreber; and it seems likely that 'The Virgin Mary Spanking the Infant Jesus' shows some awareness of the essay *A Child is being beaten*[13]. Ernst was fascinated by birds, and invented a mythical bird, Loplop/Hornebom, as his alter ego. He knew that birds, and flying, were considered to be common sexual symbols by Freud; he also knew that a vulture played a central role in *A Childhood Memory of Leonardo da Vinci*. 'A Night of Love' refers directly to Oskar Pfister's 'discovery' of a vulture in Leonardo's painting 'The Virgin and Child with St Anne', and many other works by Ernst represent birds in a similar suggestive fashion.[14]

Ernst also realised that his collage technique had certain parallels

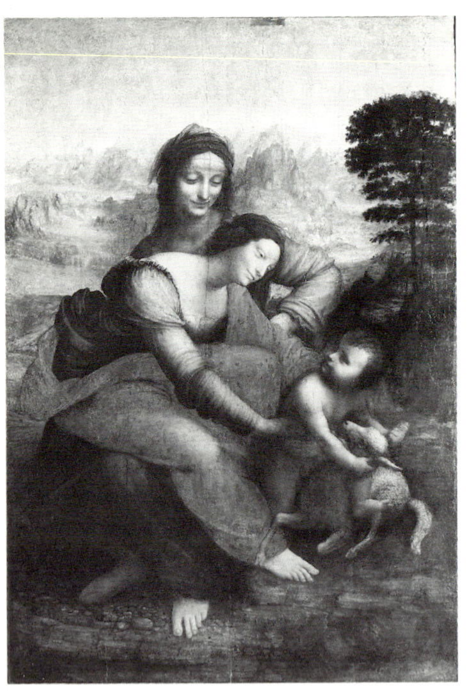

11 Leonardo da Vinci, **The Madonna and Child with St Anne**, *Musée du Louvre, Paris*

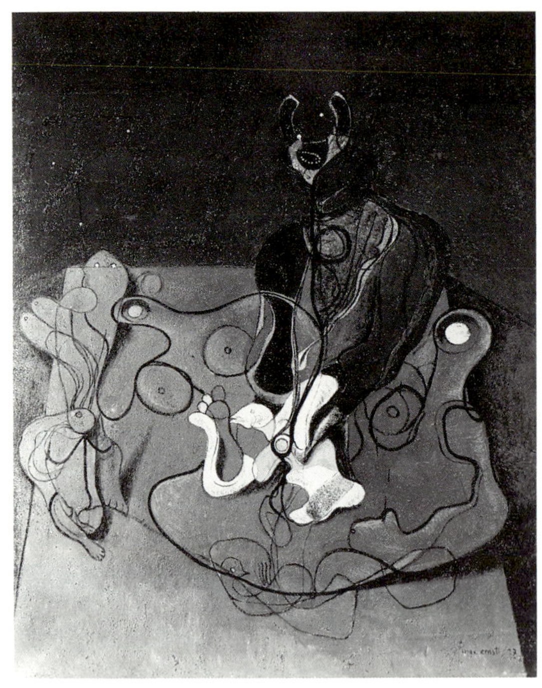

12 **Une nuit d'Amour (A Night of Love)** 1927 *Private Collection, Paris*

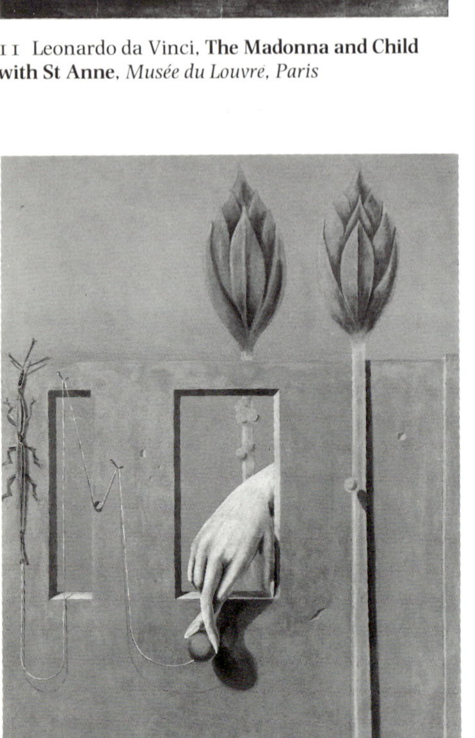

13 **Au premier mot limpide (At the First Plain Word)** 1923, oil on plaster (wall painting from the Eluards' house) *Kunstsammlung Nordrhein-Westfalen, Düsseldorf*

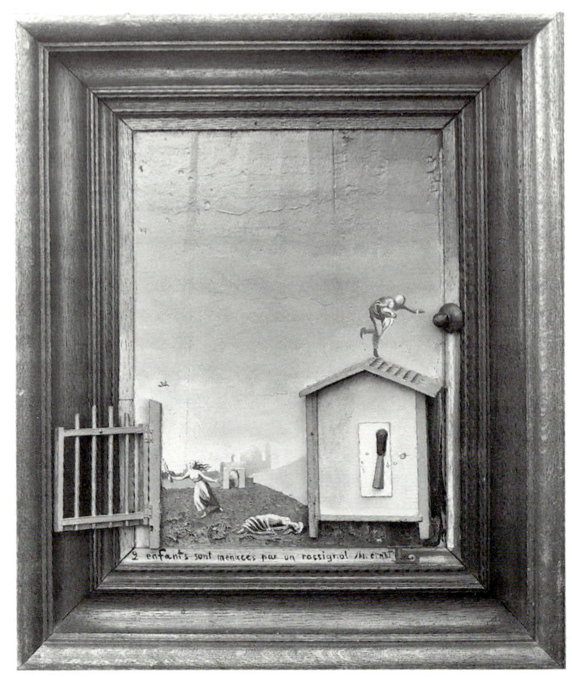

14 **Two Children are Threatened by a Nightingale** 1924 oil on wood, *Museum of Modern Art, New York*

with the 'dream work' of psychoanalytic theory. In collage – and in paintings derived from it – the artist extracted fragments from diverse available sources and assembled them to make a new image which presented anomalies and incongruities. Similarly, according to Freud, dreams use images derived from recent experience in order to construct a narrative which often appears absurd when subject to rational scrutiny, although it satisfies the sleeping subject. The idea of collage lends itself particularly well to the creation of multiple images – like, for instance, the bull-elephant-machine 'Celebes'. These exhibit one form of *condensation*, a process which Freud considered fundamental to the 'dream work'. The two fingers doubling as breasts in 'Oedipus Rex', and the crossed fingers representing a woman's legs in 'At the First Plain Word', are neat examples of Ernst's use of this device to create a double entendre in his paintings[15]. Another major characteristic of dreams in Freudian theory is *displacement*, by which elements which are fundamental to the meaning of a dream are disguised, or rendered apparently trivial, in the dream itself. An example of something similar occurring in Ernst's work can be found in 'Two Children are Threatened by a Nightingale': the bird appears as a distant image in the sky, and it is only the title that establishes its connection with the strange events in the foreground.[16]

These observable parallels between certain aspects of his work and Freud's theory of dreams do not prove that Ernst used it systematically, and it would certainly be wrong to assume this. The core of Freud's argument is that the appearance of a dream is determined by wishes which have been repressed. The meaning of a dream can only be discovered by a process of analysis in which the 'manifest content' is translated into the 'latent content', through the active participation of the dreamer, whose associations and memories contain the clues to the way in which the dream images have been constructed. This creates a suggestive model for the elaboration of paintings, but a difficult and problematic one to follow precisely. In the present context, it would only be possible to demonstrate that an artist had used such a model, and to interpret the resulting work, by having access to his or her associations connected to it, as the psychoanalyst does with a patient. Without these, the 'true' meaning of the work, if it has one, must remain a mystery.[17] Such associations are, virtually by definition, not available to the public, even if they exist. However, it is peculiarly striking about Max Ernst that he released a number of 'facts' about his life which can be interpreted rather *like* such associations in respect of pictures from the 1921–24 period. This, and related aspects of the painting itself, justifies, in my view, the hypothesis that one work of the series at least, 'Pietà or Revolution by Night', is an elaborate simulacrum of a dream, conceived in terms of Freudian theory.

Childhood Memories

I The Imitation wood panel

In 1927 Ernst published three 'Visions de demi-sommeil' in *La Révolution Surréaliste.*
The first one was titled 'between 5 and 7 years old':

> I see in front of me a panel very crudely painted with large black strokes on a red ground, imitating the grain of mahogany and provoking associations of organic forms (a menacing eye, a long nose, a large head of a bird with thick black hair etc.)
>
> In front of this panel a black and shiny man is making slow, comic, and, according to my memories of a far later period, joyously obscene gestures. This strange fellow has the moustache of my father.
>
> After executing several leaps 'in slow motion', which disgust me, with his legs apart, his knees bent, torso leaning over, he smiles and takes out of the pocket of his trousers a large pencil made out of some soft material which I have not been able to define more precisely. He sets to work: breathing loudly he hastily traces some black lines on the panel of false mahogany. He quickly gives it new, surprising, despicable forms. He exaggerates the resemblance with ferocious or slimy beasts to such an extent that they come alive, filling me with horror and anguish. Satisfied with his art, the man seizes and gathers up his creations in a sort of vase which he draws for this purpose in the air. He makes the contents of the vase turn by agitating his thick pencil faster and faster. The vase itself finishes by turning and becoming a top. The stick becomes a whip. Now I realise clearly that this strange painter is my father. He wields the whip with all his strength and accompanies his movements with terrible gasps of breath, comparable to the blasts from an enormous enraged steam engine. With his frantic efforts, he makes this abominable top turn and leap around my bed, containing all the horrors which my father is capable of summoning up, amiably, in a piece of false mahogany, with his horrible soft pencil.
>
> One day during my puberty, I considered very seriously the question of my father's conduct on the night of my conception. In response to this question of filial respect the very precise memory of this day dream surged up in my mind, which had entirely forgotten it. Since then, I have been unable to rid myself of a very unfavourable impression of my father's behaviour at the time of my conception.

As John Russell has pointed out, the first version of 'Woman, Old Man and Flower' uses elements drawn directly from this 'vision'; these were disguised when Ernst painted over the work in 1924.

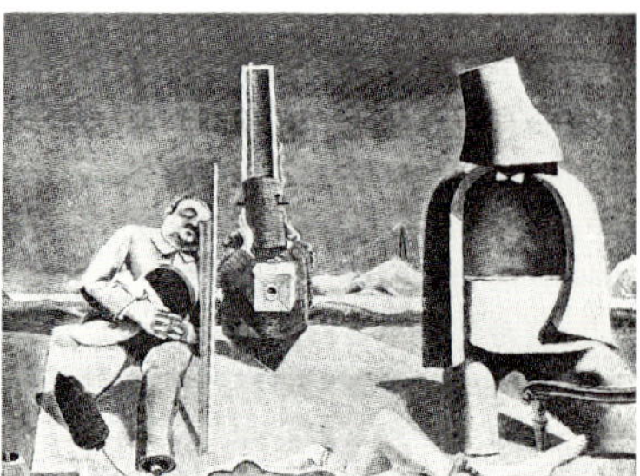

15 **Woman, Old Man and Flower I**
1923, *Overpainted*

2 Little Jesus Christ

In 1942 Ernst provided the New York review *View* with 'Some Data on the Youth of M.E. as told by himself.[19] He referred in this text to the vision of the imitation wood panel, and commented that 'Two Children are Threatened by a Nightingale' was possibly connected to it. He also mentioned another incident, which he dated to one year earlier (1896):

> To scrutinize the mystery of the telegraphic wires (and also to flee from the father's tyranny) five-year-old Max escaped from his parents' house. Blue-eyed, blond-curly-haired, dressed in a red night shirt, carrying a whip in the left hand, he walked in the middle of a pilgrim's procession. Enchanted by this charming child and believing it was the vision of an angel or even the infant of the virgin, the pilgrims proclaimed 'Look, little Jesus Christ.' After a mile or so little Jesus Christ escaped from the procession, directed himself to the station and had a long and delightful trip beside the railroad and the telegraphic wires.
>
> To appease father's fury, when the next day a policeman brought him home, little Max proclaimed that he was sure he was little Jesus Christ. This candid remark inspired the father to make a portrait of his son as a little Jesus-child, blue-eyed, blond-curly-haired, dressed in a red night shirt, blessing the world with the right hand and bearing the cross – instead of the whip – in his left.
>
> Little Max, slightly flattered by this image, had however some difficulty in throwing off the suspicion that daddy took secret pleasure in the idea of being God-the-Father, and that the hidden reason of this picture was a blasphemous pretension. Maybe Max Ernst's picture 'Souvenir de Dieu' (1923) has a direct connection with the remembrance of this fact.

These two memories are extremely suggestive in relation to the main figures represented in 'Pietà or Revolution by Night'.

The Pietà

The central feature of the painting is a strange couple: a bowler-hatted man with a prominent moustache, painted in the colour of the wall behind him, is holding a curly haired, stony, youth, dressed in a white night shirt and red trousers. The only immediate indication of their identity is provided by the title – this is a Pietà, that is, the presentation of the dead Christ by the Virgin Mary. The youth therefore 'is' Jesus and the bowler hatted man replaces his mother. This does not make ordinary sense, but it represents exactly the kind of compression of ideas and associations which Freud considered typical of dreams. The atmosphere of the painting, the different treatment of the three figures (one of whom has his eyes firmly closed) and the secondary title, 'Revolution by Night', all reinforce the impression that this is a dream.

Understood as such, the central Pietà may be related to Ernst's two childhood memories. The Christ figure recalls the little boy dressed in a red night shirt, whom his father had painted as Jesus. Logically, the man in the painting should be God, the father of Christ, since he is in the place of the mother: the figure sports a prominent moustache, like the 'father' of the 'half sleeping vision', and the second memory establishes that, in Ernst's thoughts, his father had sought to identify himself with God. So this strange Pietà represents Philippe Ernst holding his son Max. This interpretation is confirmed by two associations of a different kind: both figures relate to other paintings, one by Ernst and one by de Chirico. The youth of the 'Pietà' is in a similar pose to that adopted by Max Ernst himself in 'The Rendez-Vous of Friends', dated December 1922, while the head of the father figure is clearly modelled on de Chirico's painting of 1914 'The Child's Brain'. This painting was owned by André Breton, and has generally been interpreted as an imaginary portrait of the artist's father, for obvious reasons.

The elaboration of the central image of the 'Pietà' is therefore

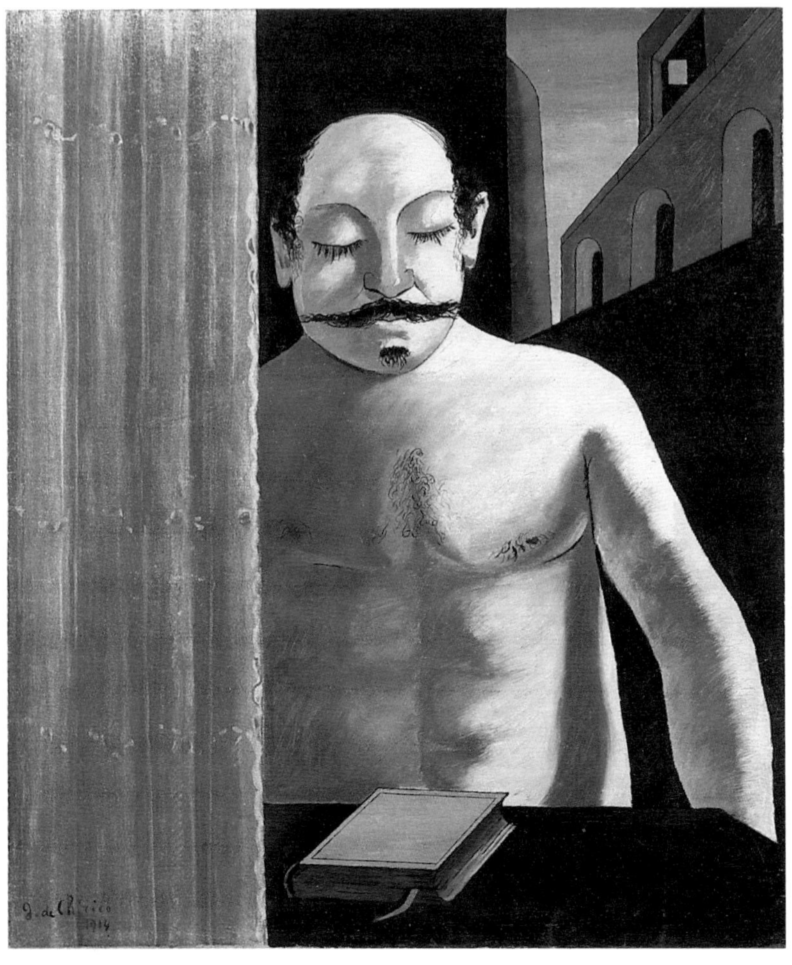

16 Giorgio de Chirico, **The Child's Brain** 1914, *Moderna Museet, Stockholm*

analogous to the mechanism of dream construction postulated by Freud in two fundamental respects: recent material from the 'dreamer's' experience (the two other paintings) has been allied to infantile material (the childhood memories) to produce a disguised representation of himself with his father. This representation incorporates both *condensation* and *displacement*: the youth combines elements of the child dressed as Jesus with the pose from the 'Rendez-Vous'; the link between the man and the father image is provided by an accessory, the moustache.

These parallels indicate that Ernst deliberately set out to incorporate Freud's ideas into his method of composition. The painting does not illustrate a dream, it represents the equivalent of a dream which the artist reasoned he could have had. Further evidence of this particular self-awareness, in Ernst's account of his childhood 'vision', leads to surprising conclusions as to the meaning of the painting.

The 'Vision de demi-sommeil' is not a vaguely obscene fantasy involving Ernst's father, but a blow by blow account of an act of sexual intercourse, employing, with some humour, symbols which correspond to typical examples cited by Freud. The wood panel, the eye, and the vase are references to the female genitals, the pencil, stick and whip are obvious phallic images, while the 'large head of a bird with thick black hair' sums up the nature of the whole noisy event.[20] Another aspect of the account also suggests a knowledge of psychoanalytic theory. According to Ernst the vision took place when he was five to seven years old; it aroused anguish and was then forgotten until the age of puberty when it resurfaced, together with a feeling of resentment against his father. This corresponds quite closely to the 'Oedipal' pattern described by Freud in the *Introductory Lectures*: fear of the father leads to sexual repression in the young child; when sexuality returns at puberty it is accompanied by hatred of the father.[21] Ernst, therefore, discovered in himself, or constructed for himself, the elements of an Oedipal past. From a Freudian perspective, however, the 'vision' has a special significance. Understood as a dream, it indicates that the child Ernst either imagined that he had, or actually did, at an earlier time, observe his parents making love, and was frightened by the experience.[22]

As a young man Ernst had understandable difficulties in his relationship with his father, who was a serious, respectable Catholic teacher. In 1920 Philippe Ernst wrote to his son and cursed him for dishonouring the family name.[23] Max had every reason, in 1922, to be pondering on the Oedipus myth. 'Pietà or Revolution by Night' does not, however, represent conflict between father and son, but the reverse, although the father figure retains some threatening associations. The painting suggests, in fact, an inverted Oedipal relationship – the son is united here not with his mother but his father.[24] This idea is reinforced by aspects of the painting's symbolism: the man has a prominent hat and tie, both of which Freud identified as symbols of the male genitalia, and the presence of the staircase indicates sexual activity.[25] Another painting of 1923 actually shows the burly father figure rushing down this staircase after a female phantom, whip in hand. In the 'Pietà' itself he is clutching his son: this strange image, in fact, expresses the 'dreamer's' wish to be made love to by his father, to be in the place of his mother, imagined or recalled in the 'half sleeping vision'.

It is possible that Ernst could have imagined this dream wish for himself, on the basis of the fascination with his father that is revealed by his childhood memories. It seems reasonable, however, to consider whether Freud's writing on the specific subject of the inverted Oedipal complex could have influenced his thinking. Freud had mentioned the topic briefly in the *Introductory Lectures*, but only produced a full theoretical discussion of it in *The Ego and the Id*, of 1923. However, one of his most famous case histories, 'From the history of an infantile neurosis', first published in 1918, was directly concerned with the ramifications of such a complex.

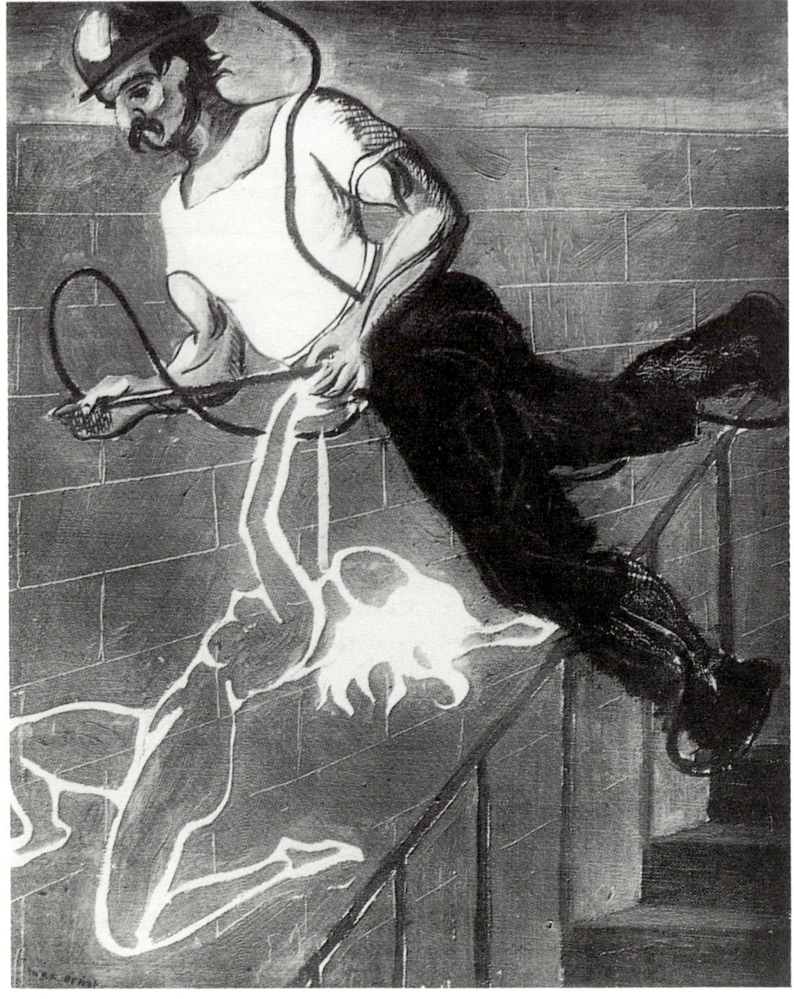

17 **Untitled** *c.*1923
Owner unknown

The Wolf Man

'From the history of an infantile neurosis' is an account and analysis of the animal phobia and obsessional neurosis experienced as a child by a man who was treated by Freud for a subsequent illness over the period 1910–14. Because of a dream which triggered the phobia, experienced when the patient was four years old, he has come to be known as 'the Wolf Man'.[26] According to Freud, the Wolf Man's childhood breakdown was caused in the first instance by an inverted Oedipal choice – he had wished to replace his mother and be loved by his father. His phobia developed as a result of the repression of this wish by his ego, and was first manifested in a dream of wolves that derived from the observation of a 'primal scene' – his parents making love when he was a baby. The phobia was gradually replaced by an obsessional neurosis concerning religion. He became very pious, to the point of identifying with Christ, but maintained a fundamentally ambivalent attitude towards God, which expressed itself in a compulsion towards blasphemy and a compensating ritual of atonement. Freud interpreted this neurosis in terms of the conflicting currents of the child's sexual life, and corresponding attitude towards his father. Christian doctrine offered a solution to his problematic love of his father, in that it allowed him to identify with Christ, whose love of God was both intense, self-sacrificing, and pure. However, the sexual aspect of his attachment surfaced in his blasphemous thoughts, which included the fantasy of bearing God a child – himself. This 'return of the repressed' also contributed to a contrary feeling towards God, of resentment and fear, which corresponded to the development of a more 'normal' Oedipal relationship to his father.[27]

I believe that the congruities between the history of the Wolf Man and the 'dream thoughts' of Ernst's 'Pietà' are such that, whether or not Ernst's childhood memories were true in substance, his elaboration of both painting and texts was dependent on the argument of Freud's essay. This, like the 'half sleeping vision', identified a 'primal scene' as the starting point of a childhood disturbance; and this, like the 'Pietà', treated the relationship of Christ to God as a symbolic representation of both conflict and desire. This may seem an extravagant theory, but there is further evidence for it in Ernst's work. The core of the Wolf Man's problems lay in his realisation that the choice made by his libido was incompatible with the narcissistic imperatives of his ego – that is, that the unacceptable price of his love for his father was castration. This realisation, Freud argued, occurred when he 'understood' what he had observed during the 'primal scene' – his mother's vagina – and related it to a castration threat made by his nurse. The wolf dream and ensuing phobia were caused by the fear this generated in him and his consequent rejection of his homosexual urge.[28] The 'Pietà', I have suggested, relates to its acceptance, and the theme of castration is not emphasised in it, although the curious shower device on the wall, painted in the same colour as the boy's shirt (but cut off from it), his undone necktie, and the fact that, as Christ, he is 'dead', may all be oblique references to this idea. Another painting of 1923, however, only makes sense when it is seen as a condensed image of this aspect of the primal scene: in 'Souvenir de Dieu' a head, with thick hair, is poised above a gaping hole, which its fingers are stroking. Not only did Ernst call this spectre a 'memory of God' – he gave the head the pointed ears and long nose of a wolf.[29]

If Ernst drew on Freud's essay to construct the 'Pietà' and related pictures, this may provide a clue to the identity of the third figure in the painting, the bearded man sketched on the wall. The head bears some resemblance to the photograph of Freud used in the first issue of *La Révolution Surréaliste*, and a reference of this kind to the inventor of

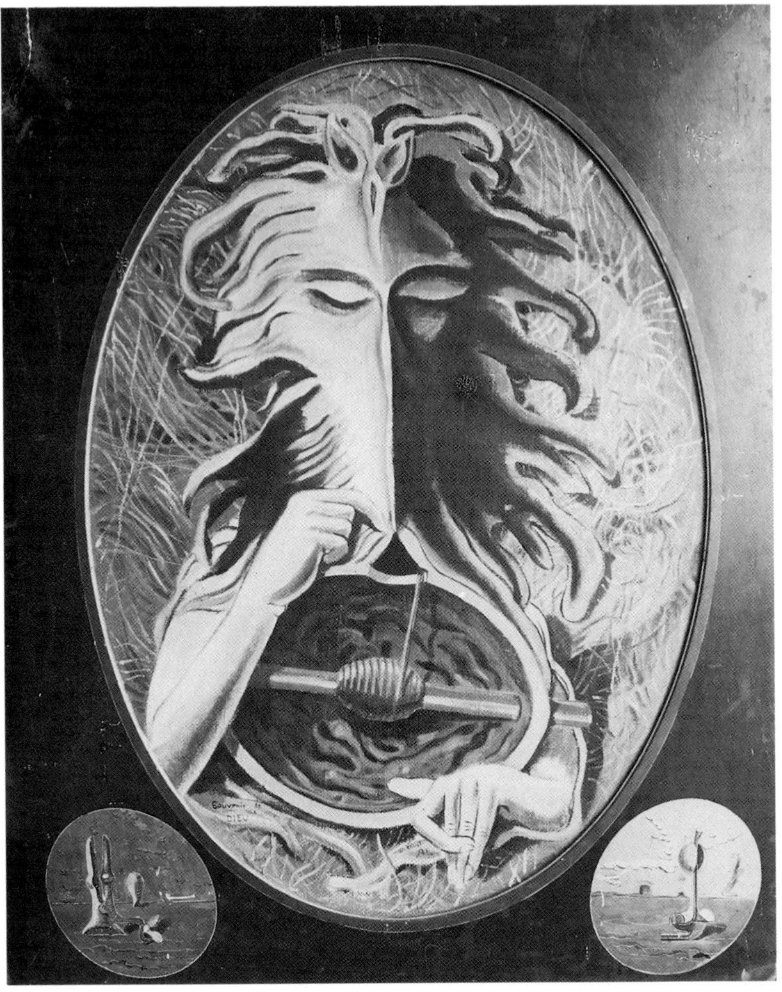

18 **Souvenir de Dieu** 1923, *Lost*

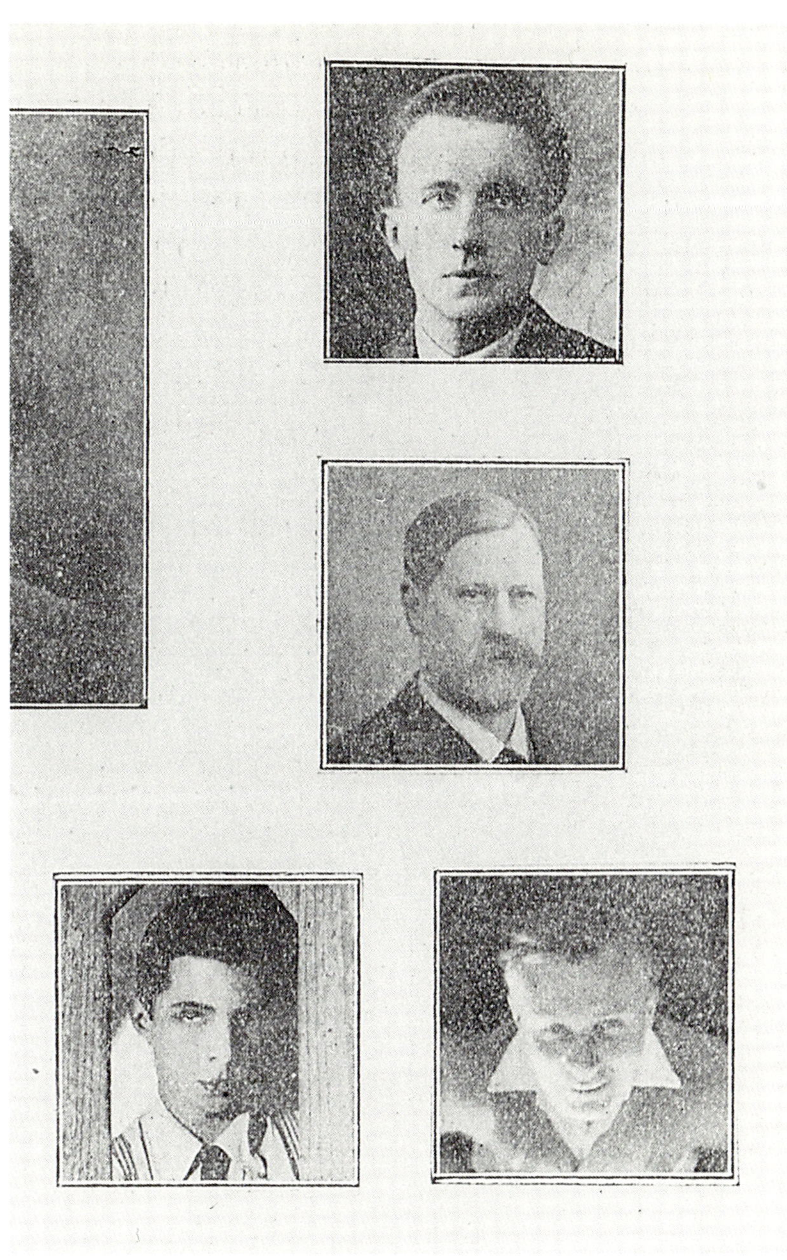

19 Photograph of Sigmund Freud (centre) from *La Révolution Surréaliste*, No.1, 1 December 1924, p. 17

psychoanalysis would certainly be appropriate to the work. If this man is Freud, however, he is almost certainly someone else as well – this is indicated by his relative youth and above all by his bandage. The 'associations' which identify the two central figures do not help much here, and Ernst has not provided others: consequently, this image stands, in some respects, outside the limits of interpretation, although its shadowy presence is important to the work.[30]

Conclusion

Most, but not all, the features of the 'Pietà' have been interpreted in this essay. It has sought to demonstrate that in this painting Ernst employed a method of composition inspired by Freud's theory of dream formation, and used a specific case history as a source. It has also suggested that several of his other paintings of the period 1921–24 function in a similar way and relate to the same specific themes. This argument raises a number of important issues. First, did Ernst really have the degree of familiarity with Freud's writings which is supposed here? The evidence for this is largely internal, but the extent of his known reading on the subject, and the intellectual qualities which pervade his art in general, make it a reasonable hypothesis. A different problem concerns the meaning of this work. Ernst's own associations suggest that the 'Pietà', like other paintings from the series, engages with his personal psyche and is based upon his difficult relationship with his father. The paintings also incorporate references of an entirely impersonal kind, in this instance, to Freud's essay on the Wolf Man. This needs to be understood in several ways: introducing specifically Freudian iconography into the material reinforced the element of detachment and calculation which was characteristic of all Ernst's work; it made the range of reference in the painting wider; it corresponded, possibly, to a wish to universalise his symbolism, in accordance with the 'myths' of his time; finally, it made the painting more complex and, in a sense, more secret. Ernst's works of this period were made, in the first instance, for himself and his friends, who often became, as in this case, their owners. In 1923 he dedicated a painting to André Breton with an explanatory caption written on the back and entitled 'Of This Men shall know Nothing'. The Surrealists believed the liberating power of creativity could be experienced by anyone, but they behaved as a group of initiates.

Why then should this painting be viewed as a masterpiece in a public gallery? In the first place, it is a particularly striking product of a set of cultural circumstances which have played a considerable part in the formation of contemporary thought, as well as being fascinating to study in their own right – the challenge to traditional norms, the search for different subject matter, and the redefinition of artistic activity, which was taken up by hundreds of painters and writers in the aftermath of the First World War. Secondly, seen in relation to its associations, the 'Pietà' possesses a remarkable intellectual elegance and bravura. But above all, the painting has a haunting power which affects anyone prepared to open their eyes and mind to it. This is a product of Ernst's disguised intention, but one which functions independently of it. The 'Pietà' does not, in fact, have to be explained in order to be understood – explanation only provides, I hope, an additional source of fascination with the work.

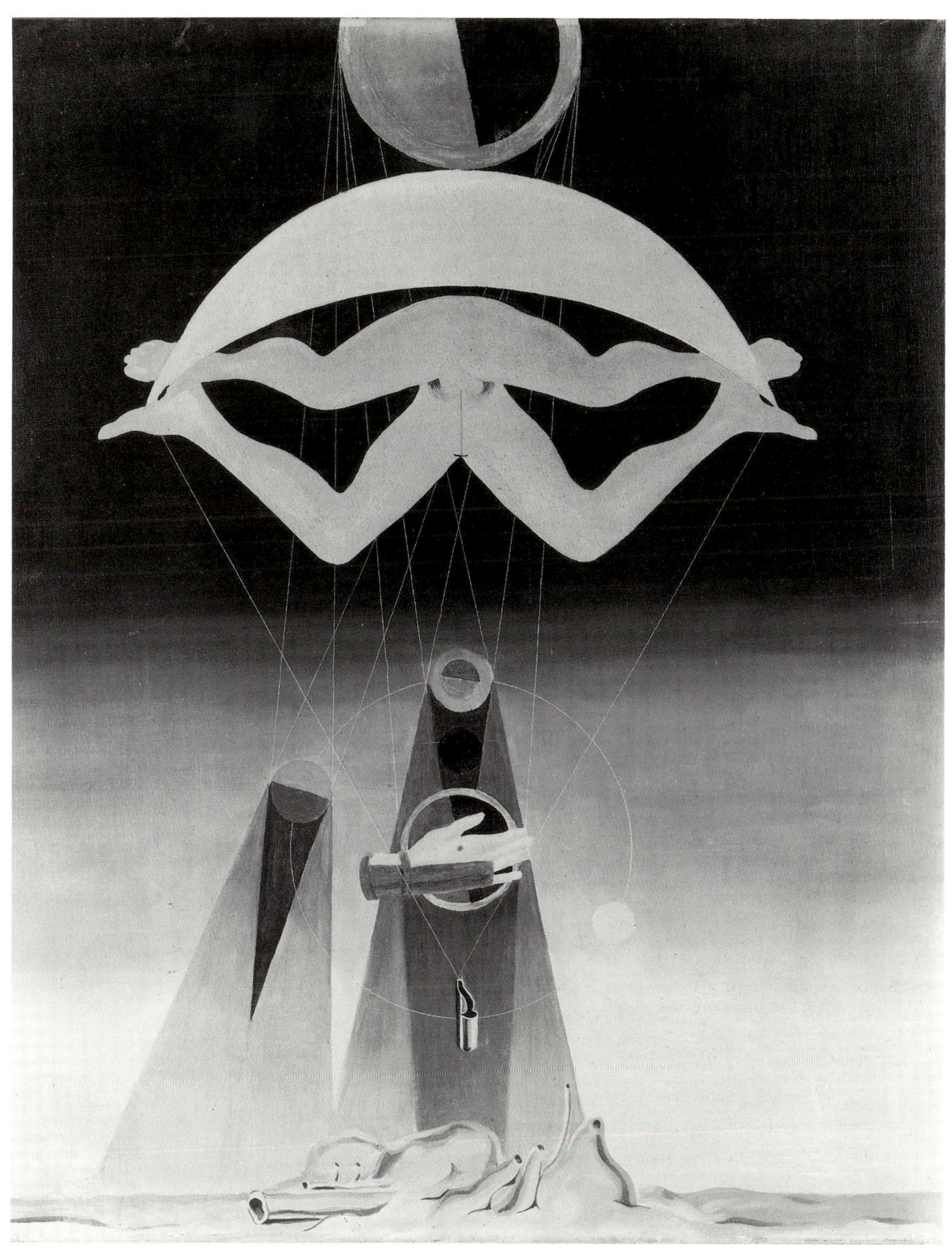

20 **Les hommes n'en sauront rien (Of This Men shall know Nothing)** 1923. *Tate Gallery*

Footnotes

1 The principal works in this series are as follows: 'Celebes', 'Oedipus Rex', 'La Belle Jardinière', 'Castor and Pollution', 'Pietà ou la Révolution la Nuit', 'Sainte Cécile', 'Ubu Imperator', 'Histoire Naturelle', 'Au Premier Mot Limpide', 'Les Hommes n'en sauront rien', 'Woman, Old Man, and Flower', and '2 Enfants sont menacés par un rossignol'. Ernst himself referred to the series in 'An Informal Life of M.E. (as told by himself to a young friend)', printed in *Max Ernst*, Tate Gallery, 1961.

2 See J. Russell, *Max Ernst* London 1967, C. Sala, *Max Ernst et la démarche onirique*, Paris 1970, W. Spies, *Die Rückkehr der schönen Gartnerin*, Cologne 1971.

3 'An Informal Life of M.E.' op. cit.

4 'Au delà de la peinture', *Cahiers d'Art* 1937, translated in *Beyond Painting*, New York 1948, p.12. For Ernst's use of collage, see W. Spies, *Max Ernst Collagen: Inventar und Widerspruch*, Cologne 1974.

5 'Celebes' uses a photograph of a grain store in the Sudan – see R. Penrose's essay in this series. Besides its derivation from *L'Invention*, 'Oedipus Rex' also uses an image, of fingers holding a nut, from *La Nature* – Spies, *Max Ernst Collagen*, ill. D 570.

6 The connection between 'Une Nuit d'amour' and Leonardo is pointed out in J. Siegel, 'Max Ernst's: One Night of Love', *Artsmagazine* 57 no.5, Jan. 1983, pp.112–15.

7 M. Sanouillet, *Dada à Paris*, Paris 1965, pp.248, 289, 368; Spies, *Max Ernst Collagen*, pp.89–100, 109–11.

8 'L'Entrée des médiums', *Littérature*, 6, November 1922, reprinted in A. Breton, *Les Pas Perdus*, Paris 1924 (1970). The others were: Benjamin Péret, Robert Desnos, René Crevel, Paul Eluard, Francis Picabia and Breton himself. Breton had written a book with Philippe Soupault in 1919 using the technique of automatic writing – *Les Champs Magnétiques* – which Ernst had apparently read.

9 Breton mentions painters in a footnote to the manifesto, notably Ernst, Picasso '(by far the purest)', Klee, Masson 'so close to us' and de Chirico 'for so long admirable'. The Surrealists did not finally despair of de Chirico until he returned to Paris in 1925.

10 For a discussion of Ernst's position in relation to the vexed issue of Surrealism and painting, see W. Spies, *Max Ernst: Loplop*, London 1983, pp. 68–75.

11 *Littérature* started publishing accounts of dreams in March 1922. The first issue of *La Révolution Surréaliste* included dreams by Breton and de Chirico. Louis Aragon called his account of the origins of Surrealism 'Une Vague de rêves', *Commerce*, 2, Paris autumn 1924.

12 Breton published a disappointed account of his interview in *Littérature* – see *Les Pas Perdus* (1970) pp.99–100. For Gradiva see W. Chadwick, *Myth in Surrealist Painting*, UMI Press 1980, chapter V. See also D. Ades, 'Freud and Surrealist Painting' in *Freud: the man, his world, his influence*, J. Miller (ed.), London 1972.

13 Spies, *Die Rückkehr der schönen Gartnerin*, pp.44–54; G. Hinton, *Burlington Magazine* May 1975; the possible reference to 'A Child is being beaten' was suggested to me by A. Eastlake of Manchester Polytechnic.

14 For Ernst's interest in Leonardo see W. Spies, *Max Ernst: Loplop*, p.100.

15 In his early collages, he used it verbally, as in the title 'Phallustrade'. He defined this, in 'Au delà de la peinture' as 'an alchemic product, composed of the following elements: the autostrade, the ballustrade, and a certain quantity of phallus' (*Beyond Painting*, p.16). W. Spies suggests that Ernst's work of the Dada period may have been more influenced by Freud's book on jokes than by *The Interpretation of Dreams* (*die Rückkehr*, pp.38–44). I am grateful to Karen Beed for pointing out the crossed legs of 'At The First Plain Word'.

16 This work is analysed, with probably too much assurance, by C. Sala, op. cit. p.48.

17 This is pointed out by W. Spies in a very thorough discussion of Ernst's use of Freud: *Max Ernst Collagen*, pp.180–82. He is sceptical of the validity of interpretations based on a Freudian reading, and his argument should be read by anyone seeking to obtain a balanced view on this issue. See also W. Spies, *Loplop*, pp.99–101, 112–14.

18 'Visions de demi-sommeil', *La Révolution Surréaliste*, 9–10, October 1927. The version of the first 'day dream' which Ernst published in *Cahiers d'Art* in 1937 (special number 'Au delà de la peinture') made the link between the man and the figure in the 'Pietà' clearer by stating that he had the '*turned-up* moustache of my father.'

19 *View*, 2, no.1, April 1942. Reprinted in *Beyond Painting*.

20 Freud listed a number of standard dream symbols in *The Interpretation of Dreams*; this was considerably expanded in the *Introductory Lectures* of 1915–16, lecture 10. The following correlations use the text of *Dreams* where possible – usually the precise example was retained in the later text. References are to the *Standard Edition* of Freud's writings, volumes III, IV, XV and XVI.
a panel – *Dreams* p.355: '"Wood" seems, from its linguistic connections, to stand in general for female "Material"'.

a menacing eye – *Dreams* p.359: 'the genitals can also be represented in dreams by other parts of the body (. . .) the female genital orifice by the mouth or an ear or even an eye.'

a sort of vase – *Lectures* p.156: 'The female genitals are symbolically represented by all such objects as share the characteristic of enclosing a hollow space which can take something into itself, by pits, cavities, and hollows, for instance, by vessels and bottles' (The French edition of the *Lectures* uses the same word as Ernst here, 'vase' where the English edition gives 'vessel'.)

pencil, stick, whip – *Lectures* p.155: 'A no less obvious aspect of the organ explains the fact that pencils, pen holders, nail files, hammers, and other instruments are undoubted male sexual symbols.' *Dreams* (added in 1919) p.380: 'Whips, sticks, lances and similar objects are familiar to us as phallic symbols.'

the large head of a bird with thick black hair – *Dreams* p.394: 'The close connection of flying with the idea of birds explains how it is that in men flying dreams usually have a grossly sensual meaning. 'See also *Dreams* p.583 – 'vögeln' means 'to fuck'.

terrible gasps of breath – this is an obvious transposition of the father's noisy breathing during intercourse. Freud made a similar analysis of 'The Wolf Man's' obsession with breathing – *Standard Edition*, XVII, p.67.

21 *Introductory Lectures*, lecture 21.

22 Freud believed that day dreams follow virtually identical rules as dreams themselves (*Dreams* p.452). The conclusion that in such a case the child had actually witnessed intercourse between the parents was virtually ineluctable. The issue is discussed at length in 'From the history of an infantile neurosis' (see below); see also *Introductory Lectures* pp.369–70.

23 'Notes pour une biographie', Max Ernst, *Ecritures*, Paris 1970, p.42. It is worth noting that Max had a son himself that same year.

24 This was noted by D. Ades in *Dada and Surrealism Reviewed*, Arts Council of Great Britain, London 1978, entry 8.12. She also suggested another source for the image of the boy. In one of the group trance sessions, Desnos identified Ernst as 'the white blouse of Fraenkel at the Salpetrière'.

25 Hats – *Dreams* pp.355, 360–1; Neckties – *Dreams* p.356; Staircases – *Dreams* p.355.

26 First published in Freud, *Sammlung Kleiner Schriften*, 4, 1918; reprinted in 5, 1922 (*Standard Edition*, XVII, pp.3–123).

27 op. cit. pp.61–8, 82–6, 114–17.

28 op. cit. p.46: 'For now he saw with his own eyes the wound of which his Nanya had spoken, and understood that its presence was a necessary condition of intercourse with his father.' p.86: 'There is no doubt whatever that at this time his father was turning into the terrifying figure that threatened him with castration. The cruel God with whom he was then struggling (. . .) threw back his character onto the patient's father.' See also pp.37–9. Freud's argument depended on the postulate that the parents had made love '*a tergo*' (i.e. back to front and upright). The soundness of his reasoning is not, of course, an issue here.

29 I am grateful to my colleague J. Steward for pointing out this last detail, and also for drawing my attention to the possible importance of Dostoevsky to a reading of the 'Pietà'. With due caution, it is worth pointing out that the case of the Wolf Man contains a passage which is suggestive in relation to 'Oedipus Rex'. At the time when the child was developing his fear of castration he had an hallucination that he had cut right through the little finger of one of his hands with his pocket knife, while playing in the garden and carving in the bark of a walnut tree (op. cit. p.85).

30 In my original essay on the 'Pietà', I suggested that the 'dream thoughts' of the painting associated this figure with Ivan Karamazov. This has a certain elegant plausibility – Ernst placed himself on Dostoevsky's knees in 'The Rendez-Vous of Friends'; *The Brothers Karamazov* is concerned with parricide; Ivan, the intellectual atheist, dreams an argument with the Devil, and tries to recover from it by tying a bandage round his head (Book XI, chapter IX). Moreover, in 1923, Ernst was living a somewhat Dostoevskian existence with Paul and Gala Eluard, who was Russian, like the Wolf Man. However, this argument does not have the same solidity as the central one concerning the 'Pietà' couple. Professor R. Pincus-Witten and Mrs Gabrielle Keiller, independently, have suggested that the figure refers to Apollinaire. The association here is with Apollinaire's trepanning, and de Chirico's 'prophetic' portrait of him. The Surrealists were indebted to Apollinaire and recognised the fact: he figured in Breton's dream, published in *La Révolution Surréaliste*, no.1. However, I find it difficult to relate Apollinaire to what I consider to be the theme of the painting.

Biographical Outline

Accounts of Ernst's life must start with his own versions of it, in 'Au Delà de la peinture', *Cahiers d'Art* 11, no. 6–7, 1937; 'Some Data on the Youth of M.E., as told by himself', *View* 2 no.1, 1942 (both reprinted in *Beyond Painting*, New York 1948); and 'An informal life of M.E. as told to a young friend', in *Max Ernst*, New York, Museum of Modern Art 1961. See also 'Notes pour une biographie' in *Max Ernst Ecritures*, Paris 1970.

1891
Born in Brühl in the Rhineland, the eldest child of Louise and Philippe Ernst. His father taught in a school for deaf and dumb children, and was a keen amateur painter.

1897
Death of a sister, Maria. Occurrence of the 'imitation wood panel' vision. 'Fear of death and the annihilating powers' ('Some Data').

1906
Death of his pet cockatoo, Hornebom, and birth of a young sister. 'The *perturbation* of the youth was so enormous that he fainted. . . . A series of mystical crises, fits of hysteria, exaltations and depressions followed. A dangerous confusion between birds and humans became encrusted in his mind and asserted itself in his drawings and paintings.' ('Some Data')

1909
Registered at the University of Bonn. Followed courses in philosophy, psychiatry, and art history.

1910/11
Met August Macke.

1913
Exhibited with the *Rheinische Expressionisten* in Bonn, and at the 'First German Autumn Salon', Der Sturm Gallery, Berlin.

1914
Met Hans Arp

1914–18
Served in the Artillery.

1916
On leave, exhibited at the Der Sturm Gallery, Berlin, and met G. Grosz and J. Heartfield.

1918
Married Louise Strauss, an art historian and journalist.

1919–20
Joined Young Rhineland group. Met J. Baargeld (A. Grünwald) and engaged with him and, intermittently, Hans Arp in a number of Dada activities in Cologne. Made contact with Tzara in Zurich, visited Munich and met Paul Klee. Discovered the work of de Chirico and began making collages. Birth of a son, Jimmy.

1921
Exhibition at Au Sans Pareil, Paris. Met the Bretons and the Eluards. Collaboration with Paul Eluard. Painted the 'Elephant from Celebes'.

1922
(Autumn) moved to Paris.

1923–24
Participation in Surrealist activities. Completed the 'dream' series of pictures.

1924
With Gala, retrieved Paul Eluard from his 'flight' to the Far East.

1925
Discovered the technique of *frottage*; produced *Histoire Naturelle*.

1926
One man show at the Galerie Van Leer, Paris.

1927
Published three 'Visions de demi-sommeil' in *La Révolution Surréaliste*.

1928
Married Marie-Berthe Aurenche.

1929
Published *La femme 100 têtes* – his first collage novel.

1930
Exhibited in the collage exhibition at the Galerie Goemans, Paris. Began the Loplop series. Published his second collage novel *Rêve d'une petite fille qui voulut entrer au Carmel.*

1932
First exhibition in New York, at the Julien Levy Gallery.

1933
Condemned by the Nazi regime.

1934
Third collage novel, *Une Semaine de Bonté.*

1937
Special Ernst issue of *Cahiers d'Art.* Met Leonora Carrington at the International Surrealist exhibition in London.

1938
Break with André Breton after the 'excommunication' of Paul Eluard.

1939–41
Interned as an enemy alien, released, reinterned – finally allowed to cross the frontier into Spain and escape to the USA, with the help of Alfred Barr and Peggy Guggenheim. Marriage to Peggy Guggenheim after entry of the USA into the war.

1942
Special Ernst number of *View.*

1943
Met Dorothea Tanning and moved to Arizona.

1946
Married Dorothea Tanning.

1948
Publication of *Beyond Painting* in Documents of Modern Art series, edited by Robert Motherwell. Became an American citizen.

1949
Published *At Eye Level/Paramyths.*

1950
Visited Paris; exhibited at Galerie René Drouin.

1953
Settled in Paris.

1954
Grand Prix at the Venice Biennale.

1955
Moved to the Touraine, with Dorothea Tanning.

1958
Became a French citizen.

1961
Retrospective exhibition at the Museum of Modern Art, New York.

1962
Retrospective exhibition in Cologne.

1964
Published *Maximiliana ou l'exercice illégal de l'astronomie.*

1969
Retrospective exhibition in Stockholm.

1975
Full retrospective exhibition in New York (Solomon R. Guggenheim Museum) and Paris (Grand Palais).

1976
Died in Paris.

Select Bibliography

Ernst's Writings

Beyond Painting, New York, 1948.

Ecritures, Paris, 1970.

Monographs etc.

Russell, John, *Max Ernst*, London, 1967.

Schneede, Uwe M., *The Essential Max Ernst*, London, 1972.

Spies, Werner, *Max Ernst Collagen: Inventar und Widerspruch*, Cologne, 1974.

Spies, Werner and Metken, S. & G., *Max Ernst Oeuvre Katalog*, Cologne, 1975, 1976 and 1979.

Spies, Werner, *Max Ernst: Loplop*, Munich 1982, London 1983.

Acknowledgements

I have benefited from the comments and encouragement of my colleagues Kenneth McConkey, John Milner and Jill Steward, and of Professor R. Pincus-Witten of the City University of New York. I am, like all writers on Max Ernst, indebted to the scholarship of Werner Spies. I am also grateful to the editor of *Artsmagazine*, New York, Richard Martin, for publishing the article on which this essay is based (*Artsmagazine*, March 1981).